Walking Boldly in the Assignment God Entrusted to You

Walking Boldly in the Assignment God Entrusted to You

SHAMEKA NICOLE

Published by: *Visionaire Publishing & Consulting*
www.visionairepc.com
info@visionairepc.com

ISBN: 979-8-9944318-4-9

Printed in the United States of America

CONTENTS

Dedication 1

Introduction 3

Before Reading 11

1. Where Are You? 19
2. Called to Build, Not Just Believe 37
3. The Confidence Struggle No One Talks About 55
4. The Cost of Not Showing Up 71
5. The Decision to Go Forward 87
6. Kingdom Stewardship 103

7. When God Calls You For Such a Time as This 121

8. Faith Requires Action 137

9. Continue to Do the Work 151

10. Already Started But Stalled 165

11. It's Time to Show Up, Now Walk it Out 189

Epilogue 201

Now It's Your Turn 207

About the Author 213

Connect With Me 215

Also by Shameka 217

Dedication

This book is for the ones who almost quit. For the visionaries who heard God clearly but wrestled with confidence. For the leaders who delayed, not out of disobedience, but fear of getting it wrong. For the builders who kept showing up even when clarity felt distant.

Most of all, this book is dedicated to God, who trusted me with the vision, carried me through the process, and kept calling me forward when I wanted to pull back.

If this book finds you where I once stood, let it remind you that your yes still matters and that it is time to show up.

Introduction

This is for you, if you've heard God's voice, but fear has held you back. Maybe you know you're being called to something, but the weight of it all is overwhelming. You feel the responsibility, the stretching, and it's scary. This is also for you, if you're aware that what God is asking of you means stepping out of your comfort zone.

This book is for the believer who knows God has spoken but has not yet moved. It is for the faith-driven entrepreneur who launched with vision but quietly stalled somewhere between the promise and the process. It is for the leader who carries responsibility in one hand and self-doubt in the other. It is for the ministry worker, the business owner, the person in a nine-to-five who senses there is more, and the visionary who has been preparing so long that preparation has become its own form of hiding. Wherever you are in your journey, whether you are just beginning to hear God's voice or you have been hearing it for years and still have not fully responded, this book was written for you. The call to show up does not belong to one type of person. It belongs to anyone who has said yes to God and is still learning what that yes requires.

There comes a point when excuses lose their power. You realize you heard Him clearly, and avoiding the next step is no longer an option. I have stood in that place more than once.

We all have our own unique journey, but one thing remains the same. We're all called to show up and be faithful. When God speaks to us, we're faced with a choice. We can either respond and take a step of faith, or we can retreat and play it safe. For me, one of the defining moments was when I felt God nudging me to become an entrepreneur. At first, it was exhilarating, but it wasn't about following the latest trend. It was about obeying God's voice, even when it felt uncertain. I knew that this path wouldn't be easy, that my income might fluctuate, and that stability would look different from one month to the next. Some seasons would be abundant, while others would be marked by uncertainty. But if this was truly God's direction for my life, then I knew I had to trust Him, even when the outcome was far from guaranteed. It required me to move forward in faith, to take risks, and to trust that God would provide and guide me every step of the way.

God reminded me of earlier assignments I completed faithfully. He also revealed where I shifted along the way. I will unpack that later.

What became clear is that when God entrusts you with purpose, He also entrusts you with people and influence. That responsibility has weight and shows up through conversations that require wisdom and moments that call for leadership.

There were times I could not ignore what God was placing in my spirit. In the middle of everyday life, something would rise within me so strongly that I had to pause and capture it in the *Notes* section in my phone. I refused to treat those moments casually and knew that what He released mattered. Those notes became prayers, strategies, warnings, and direction. And one question kept coming to mind: *When is it time to go forward?*

That question stretches you because movement requires action. It demands visibility. It forces you to step forward without hiding behind readiness. Faith must become active.

In 2024, I found myself at a crossroads, and that's what led me to my very first FinisHER Conference. It was like everything falling into place. The theme scripture was Hebrews 12:1-2 and it really stuck with me. It's all about letting go of the things that weigh us down and running the race that's set before us with endurance, all while keeping our eyes fixed on Jesus.

What happened during that gathering was really something. God had shared some things with me privately, but then they were confirmed in front of everyone. I felt so much stronger and clearer about everything afterwards. *Yet confirmation does not eliminate opposition.*

The day after was like being in the middle of a war zone. I was all confused and unsure about things that had seemed so clear before. The pressure was really strong, making it hard to feel like I was getting anywhere. But I learned something important during that time: *when God says something, there's usually a fight that comes after*. I knew what He instructed me to do, yet doing so required courage.

I used to doubt my own voice, even when it was speaking with confidence and authority. I would downplay my influence, even when I knew God was backing me up. And I would put off making decisions, even when I had all the tools and wisdom I needed to make them.

When you're trying to finish what God has given you to do, be ready for some pushback. You'll face things like doubt, feeling tired, and being confused. These will try to get in your way. The enemy isn't always obvious, sometimes it's just a slow wearing down, a little discouragement here and there, trying to make you give up. I want you aware and prepared to stand firm.

This book came to be in the space where knowing what to do and actually doing it didn't quite meet. It was a moment of realization that I wasn't waiting for God to make a move. He was waiting for me to take a step. These pages come from lived experience. Obedience. Reluctance. Growth. Real faith tested in real moments.

As you dive into this, get ready for real talk about being brave, leading with purpose, and using what you have to make a difference. You'll find truth from the Bible and practical advice to help you become the leader you're meant to be. And when fear is pretending to be wisdom, expect a gentle but firm push to help you see things clearly. Above all, expect clarity.

This book exists because obedience demanded it. I learned that saying yes is not enough. You must *live* in the yes.

Before you continue, consider this:

- What have you postponed that God already confirmed?
- Where are you over-preparing instead of advancing?

- What shifts if you fully embrace what He entrusted to you?

- What waits on the other side of your obedience?

If He has given you the signal, *it is time to show up.*

Before Reading

Take a deep breath and stop for a second. Be really honest with yourself right now, before you move on.

What's going on with you? Have you been hiding from something or someone? It feels like fear is really loud right now, doesn't it? You're probably wondering why you're doubting things that God already made pretty clear. The question is, do you really trust the God who chose you for this moment, or are doubts and past experiences starting to override what He's saying? It's like, whose voice are you listening to. God's or the voices of fear and uncertainty?

I ask these questions because I have been there. I struggled with fear that came from old wounds, rejection, and voices that were never sent by God. Things I experienced in my past tried to shape how I saw myself and how I responded to the call on my life. Over time, those things created hesitation and made me question whether I was really equipped to do what God was asking of me. But I want you to know you do not have to stay stuck in that place. You do not have to shrink back when God is calling you forward. You do not have to play it safe or hide behind labels, excuses, or lies that were never meant to define you.

Before you go any further, I want to invite you into a moment of repentance. Not the kind that brings shame, but the kind that brings alignment.

Prayer of Repentance

Father, I repent for the times I let fear take over instead of trusting You. I repent for doubting what You were telling me and questioning what You made clear. I regret not being brave when You asked me to take a step forward, and I'm sorry for believing things that weren't true, things that You never said. Please forgive me for choosing what was easy over doing what You wanted me to do, and for hesitating instead of trusting You. I ask You to help me see things the way You do, and to remind me of who I am because of You. Help me think clearly, calm my fears, and give me the confidence to move forward, doing what You want me to do. I ask this in Jesus' name.

As you've prayed, take a moment to breathe deeply and let the grace of repentance wash over you. This isn't about dwelling on past mistakes or shortcomings, but about embracing the restoration and realignment that God is doing in your life right now. Repentance is a powerful catalyst for change, paving the way for newfound movement, clarity, and courage. I want to be honest with you. I've had to pray a similar prayer myself, confronting my own fears, doubts, and hesitations before I could move forward in obedience to God's will. That moment of raw honesty with Him marked a significant turning point in my life, and I believe it can do the same for you. By acknowledging our weaknesses and surrendering them to God, we open ourselves up to a fresh outpouring of His grace and a deeper sense of purpose. Remember, repentance isn't just about looking back, but about moving forward with renewed hope and confidence in God's plan for your life.

I was going through a tough time, and God made me stop and think about my life. It was like a wake-up call where I saw all the times I had let fear hold me back and didn't trust Him enough. He showed me the moments when I should have been braver and more obedient. As I looked back, He reminded me of my true identity and the purpose He had for me. It was a powerful moment, where I realized I needed to step up and be the person He created me to be.

I hope this book has a similar impact on you, encouraging you to step into the roles and situations that God has planned for you. May it help you understand the power and identity that's yours, even on days when you don't feel entirely prepared or equipped.

Are you prepared to take a step forward and see what's waiting for you? There are people who are connected to your actions and opportunities that will only come to life when you say *yes*. On the other side of your willingness to move forward, you'll find a sense of purpose that's been waiting for you all along. So, before we go any further, I have to ask if you are ready to show up and see what happens?

It's
Time
TO
SHOW UP

Chapter 1

Where Are You?

There's a question that needs to be answered truthfully. It's a question that gets to the heart of things: *where are you, really?* This is one of the first things God asked people, way back in the book of Genesis. You see, after Adam and Eve disobeyed God and tried to hide, the Bible says God called out to them, "Where are you?" Now, God wasn't asking because He didn't know where they were. He knew exactly where they had gone. What He was doing was inviting them to think about where they had put themselves, to recognize the choice they had made. It's like He was saying, "Okay, you've made a decision, now own up to it, and let's talk about where you are." This question, "Where are you?" is still one we need to answer today, and it's not just about our physical location, but about where we are in our lives, and in our relationship with God.

To move forward, you need to know your current situation. Not the situation you want to be in, not the situation you pretend to be in, but your *real* situation. It's about being honest with yourself and understanding where you are right now. Only then can you start making progress and moving in the right direction.

Where are you right now? Where are you in your faith? Where are you in your obedience? Where are you in your confidence? Where are you in your willingness to show up? And just as important, how did you get here? Was it fear that slowed you down? Was it disappointment that made you cautious? Was it your own thinking that talked you out of obedience? Was it a lack of discipline that turned delay into a habit? These questions are not meant to shame you. They are meant to free you.

There are moments in Scripture where God does not just ask questions. He gives direction. In Deuteronomy 2:2–3, God speaks to the children of Israel and says, "And the LORD spoke to me, saying: 'You have skirted this mountain long enough; turn northward.'"

God was essentially saying, you have been going in circles long enough. You have learned what you needed to learn here. It is time to move.

We often find ourselves stuck, but it's not because God hasn't spoken to us. We've become too comfortable with our familiar ways, the same old fears, excuses, patterns, and hesitations that hold us back. We've been circling the same mountain for far too long. But then, something changes. God breaks into our routine and says, "You've been here long enough." It's a wake-up call, a reminder that we can't stay stuck in our comfort zones forever. God is ready to move us forward, to take us to new heights and help us overcome the things that have been holding us back. The question is, are we ready to listen and respond?

I had to face that question when I realized my peace at work was gone. I carried so many concerns, yet nothing shifted. No real change. Just the same cycle. At the same time, the thought of stepping into full-time entrepreneurship kept surfacing. And every time it did, fear tried to tighten its grip. My mind filled with questions. What about my portion of the bills? What if the income was inconsistent? What if I could not cover what needed to be covered? Listen, the questions did not stop. They came one after another. And I had to decide whether I would let those questions lead me or let obedience lead me.

Even as I am editing this book on March 1, 2026, I am living the very message I wrote. I officially submitted my two week's notice to the company where I have been employed for almost four years. I would have celebrated my four-year anniversary on March 21. Instead, on Monday, February 23, I turned in my notice. I want you to understand something. This was not emotional. It was not impulsive. It was obedience.

After a prayer meeting on January 30, the Lord spoke clearly to me and told me to write my resignation letter. There was no confusion about what I heard. The instruction was simple: *Write it*. I remember sitting with that word because writing it meant I was acknowledging that a shift was coming. It meant I could not pretend I did not hear Him.

Then on February 2, I had a dream where I left my work laptop behind. It was not dramatic, but it was clear. I was walking away from what had been familiar. A few days later, on February 8, I had another detailed dream that showed me I was stepping into something new. I could sense transition. I could sense movement. It felt like God was pulling back the curtain just enough to let me know that there was more.

Those dreams were confirmation for me. God was affirming that my obedience was not misplaced. He was reminding me that this decision was rooted in alignment. Do not misunderstand me, I felt the weight of it. I thought about stability, consistency and even about what it meant to walk away just weeks before an anniversary milestone. Four years is not a small investment. But I also knew that partial obedience would cost me more than a steady paycheck ever could. So I chose to respond.

As I edit these pages about showing up, I am actively showing up in my own life. I am writing from the middle of transition. From the place where faith has to move beyond words and into action and here is what I know. When God confirms a thing, peace follows obedience. Even if the details are still unfolding, there is a steadiness that comes when you move because He said move.

This step was not about leaving a job. It was about trusting God with the next chapter. It was about believing that the same God who sustained me for four years will sustain me in what comes next.

I am not stepping into the unknown alone. I am stepping into what He already prepared. And that makes all the difference.

Now back to the story...

God does not tell the Israelites to stay and analyze the mountain. He does not tell them to camp there a little longer. He tells them to turn. Turning requires intention, movement and trust. And often, turning feels uncomfortable because it means leaving what is familiar, even if what is familiar is limiting.

Sometimes we are afraid to be honest about where we are because the truth exposes areas where our faith was weak or our discipline slipped. But God does not want you to stay in that place. He asks "Where are you?" so He can tell you where to go next. This is where the call to show up becomes real. Just as God called Peter out of the boat, He is calling you too. Peter was surrounded by wind and waves. Fear was present. Doubt was real. But Jesus did not give him a long explanation. He gave a clear invitation. "Come."

We all face moments where we have to decide whether to stay in our comfort zone or take a step of faith. For Peter, that moment came when he had to choose between staying in the boat or stepping out onto the water. The amazing thing is that the miracle didn't happen while he was still in the boat. It happened when he took that first step. And even when he started to sink, Jesus didn't leave him to struggle on his own. Instead, He reached out and caught him. That's the same kind of grace that's available to us today. God isn't expecting us to have all the answers or to feel completely confident before we take a step of faith. He's simply asking us to respond to Him, to trust Him enough to move forward, even when we're not sure what's going to happen next. He's not looking for fearlessness, but for the kind of faith that says, "I don't know what's ahead, but I know You're with me, and that's enough."

When God questions where you are, it's not about pointing fingers or laying blame. Instead, He's offering a gentle invitation to step out of the shadows and into a place of harmony with Him. And when He says "You've been here long enough," He's not trying to rush you or push you away. He's simply guiding you towards a new path, one that's in line with His plan for you. It's a call to move forward, to realign yourself with His purpose, and to trust that He's leading you to a better place.

It's time to stop going around in circles and take a step forward. We need to turn our lives around and head in a new direction.

Encouragement

If you have felt stuck, uncertain, or hesitant, hear this clearly. Awareness is the beginning of movement. God is not disappointed in you. He is directing you. You are not behind. You are being repositioned. The mountain you have been circling has served its purpose, the lesson has been learned and the season has shifted.

Affirmations

I am honest about where I am, and I am not ashamed of my journey.

God gives me clarity and direction for where to go next.

I will no longer circle what God has already addressed.

I hear God's instruction, and I respond with obedience.

Fear no longer keeps me in familiar places.

I trust God enough to turn and move forward.

I am stepping out of delay and into alignment.

Faith in Motion

Knowing where you are is important, but that alone is not the destination. Awareness is only the beginning. The real responsibility begins after God shows you something.

This week, take time to do the following:

- Set aside uninterrupted time to reflect honestly on where you are spiritually, emotionally, and practically
- Write down the areas where you feel stuck, hesitant, or unsure

- Identify one pattern or habit that has kept you circling instead of moving
- Ask God for clarity on the next step, not the entire plan
- Take one small but visible step that reflects obedience, even if it feels uncomfortable

Faith does not require you to have everything figured out. It requires movement in the direction God is pointing.

Prayer

God, I thank You for meeting me where I am. I ask You to search my heart and reveal anything that has kept me from moving forward. Show me where fear, doubt, or comfort has influenced my decisions. I surrender every excuse, every hesitation, and every place where I have chosen familiarity over obedience. Give me clarity for my next step and courage to take it. Help me trust You enough to move when You say it is time. In Jesus' name, amen.

Pause Here

Pause. Take a breath. Sit with what God just revealed to you. Do not rush past this moment. Do not explain it away. Let truth settle.

CHAPTER 2

Called to Build, Not Just Believe

After you identify where you are, the next step becomes clear. That step is to *go back and pick up what you put down.* Awareness without action keeps you stuck. Once God shows you where you are, He also expects movement. This is when what you say you believe starts requiring action.

When I say we are called to build, I am simply saying we are called to partner with God in what He is calling us to do. Building is not about striving or trying to prove anything. It is about alignment and agreeing with heaven and working alongside God instead of trying to run ahead of Him or do things on our own.

One of the greatest lessons I had to learn on this journey was how to relinquish control. There were seasons when I had ideas, plans, and good intentions, but I did not always seek God for direction. I wanted progress and movement, but I was trying to build without fully partnering with Him. That tension revealed something important. It showed me that having vision is not the same as having alignment.

God began to deal with me about the difference between building something for Him and building something with Him. Building with Him required surrender. Many believers are comfortable believing God, but uncomfortable partnering with Him. Belief feels safe because it does not require much of you. Partnership does. It requires responsibility, obedience, and consistency.

When God entrusts you with a vision or an assignment, He is inviting you into partnership. God does not give vision casually. He gives it intentionally and He expects participation.

Scripture makes this clear:

> "*For we are His workmanship, created in Christ Jesus for good works, which God prepared beforehand that we should walk in them.*"
> —Ephesians 2:10

That tells us the work was already prepared long before we recognized the call. The assignment existed before we had the words to describe it. It is not our job to come up with the work. It is our job to walk in what God already designed. He was intentional about what He placed inside of you, and He was just as intentional about the timing of when He revealed it. This is where many of us wrestle. Just because you have a calling does not mean insecurity disappears overnight. Being assigned does not cancel out fear. Seeing the vision does not automatically make you confident. Confidence is built in motion. It grows when you obey. It strengthens when you take one step, then another, even when you still feel stretched.

Walking with God is not passive. It is partnership and requires your participation. It requires your yes. It requires you trusting Him enough to move forward while He is still shaping you into who you are becoming.

Nehemiah understood this well. His story is not just about rebuilding a wall. It is about responsibility and focus. He felt the burden of what was broken, but he did not rush ahead in his own strength. He prayed, fasted and waited for God's direction. When the assignment became clear, he committed himself fully to the work.

The moment the rebuilding began, opposition followed. Tobiah and Sanballat mocked him and questioned his intentions. When mockery did not work, they attempted intimidation. When fear failed, they turned to deception. Their goal never changed. They wanted the work to stop. That same pattern shows up when we partner with God. Distractions arise. Voices question your ability. Confusion tries to make you second guess what God made clear. Fatigue sets in. Fear attempts to slow your obedience. I know this because I lived it. Every time I stepped forward in obedience, resistance followed closely behind.

When I tried to build in my own strength, confusion increased. When I slowed down and sought God, clarity returned. That pattern taught me that success was never about effort alone. It was about partnership and alignment.

Nehemiah built with prayer and strategy. He stayed alert but committed. He acknowledged the opposition, but he did not allow it to stop the assignment. That is the posture God is calling us to take. Resistance is not proof that you missed God. Many times, it is confirmation that the work matters.

If you are feeling pressure or internal resistance, it does not mean you are disqualified. You were not called just to believe. You were called to partner with God. You were given vision to steward it with obedience. And you are not expected to do it alone.

Before you move forward, ask yourself honestly:

- Am I partnering with God or trying to build on my own?
- Have distractions pulled me away from the work I was called to do?
- Have I mistaken resistance for disqualification?

God is not asking you to be perfect. He is asking you to participate. He is not waiting for you to feel fearless. He is waiting for your *yes*. The work has already been prepared. The invitation has already been extended. You were never called to believe from a distance. You were called to engage, to partner, to build alongside Him. Showing up is not a one-time moment. It is a decision you make again and again. And one of the first ways you show up is by choosing to partner with God in what He has already trusted you with and already called you to do. The question is are you willing to show up?

Encouragement

What God called you to build will be completed. The distractions sent to delay you will not derail you. The assignment on your life is protected by heaven.

Just as Nehemiah finished the wall, you will finish the work.

Affirmations

I am called to build with God.

I partner with Him in every decision.

I do not come down from the work He assigned me.

I am focused, faithful, and equipped.

What God started through me, He will bring to completion.

You are assured. You are aligned. You are appointed. Now keep building.

Faith in Motion

There is something powerful about admitting that you are not called to create the vision from scratch. You are called to steward what God already designed.

- Write down what God has called you to build.
- Identify one way you have been observing instead of participating.
- Take one step that moves the vision from idea to action this week.

Prayer

God, I surrender the need to do this in my own strength. I release the pressure to prove myself or rush Your timing. Teach me how to build with You. Not ahead of You. Not without You. With You. Search my heart and reveal where fear has delayed obedience. Strengthen me where I feel inadequate and remind me that You equip those You call. Align my thoughts with Your truth and my steps with Your will. Give me discernment to know when to move and when to wait.

Help me steward what You have entrusted to me with humility and boldness. Let my work honor You. Where doubt whispers, speak louder. Where I feel weak, renew my strength. I do not want to build something impressive. I want to build something obedient. I choose to participate fully. I choose to trust You. I choose to move in faith. In Jesus' name, Amen.

Pause Here

Pause. Sit with this. Let God show you what building with Him really looks like.

It's
Time
TO
SHOW UP

CHAPTER 3

The Confidence Struggle No One Talks About

What God is calling you to do is already in you. That truth took me a long time to fully accept. I struggled with trusting myself to carry what God gave me. I never questioned His power, His wisdom, or His ability. I believed without hesitation that God could do anything. What I wrestled with was believing that He could truly use me as I was, with my history, my personality, my voice, and my past. That is where the real confidence battle showed up for me, and the enemy knows that too.

One of his most effective tactics is not trying to convince us that God cannot do it. Instead, he plants the question: *God, did You really choose the right one?* That question opens the door to comparison and insecurity. It pulls up old memories, past mistakes, and seasons where you felt overlooked or unqualified. The enemy loves to use your past as evidence against your future, even after God has redeemed it. I have watched this play out in my own life more times than I can count.

Confidence struggles do not always show up as fear. Sometimes they look like overpreparing, hoping that more work will finally quiet the doubt. Sometimes they look like overthinking, replaying conversations and decisions long after God already gave clarity. Sometimes they look like delaying decisions you were already graced to make and sometimes they look like hiding behind busyness, staying active so you never have to stand exposed in obedience. Fear does not always tell you no. Sometimes it simply says, wait a little longer.

2 Timothy 1:7 reminds us, *"For God has not given us a spirit of fear, but of power and of love and of a sound mind."* Fear often disguises itself as wisdom, but wisdom produces movement, while fear produces hesitation.

I am drawn to the way God calls people who do not feel confident at all. Moses is one of the clearest examples. When God called him, Moses immediately focused on what he believed disqualified him. His past, speech and limitations. He questioned whether God had chosen the wrong person. When God pushed back, Moses asked for help. He asked for Aaron to speak for him. God allowed Aaron to be his mouthpiece, but Moses was still the one God called.

God's response to Moses included one powerful question: *What is in your hand?* God was not asking Moses to go find something new. He was pointing him back to what he already had. The staff in Moses' hand was familiar, ordinary, and overlooked, but it became the very tool God used to perform miracles. That staff was a weapon. It was evidence that God equips what He calls.

I pose the same question! *What is in your hand? What gift, experience, voice, skill, or testimony have you been downplaying because it feels too simple or too common?* What God placed in your hand is your weapon. That is the tool God is going to use. Do not discredit it. Do not minimize it. Do not overlook it because it does not look like someone else's.

I learned this lesson in a very personal way when God called me to host my first conference. When the vision first came, I was excited and ready to move. I told my Pastor and my best friend about it so they could hold me accountable. But as the date approached, excitement slowly gave way to doubt. I started questioning whether I was truly equipped to carry and deliver the message God gave me. I wondered if my voice was enough and if God could really use me in that way. That lack of confidence led me to ask someone I deeply respect to co-host with me. At the time, it felt wise. It felt safe. It felt like support. But if I am honest, it was rooted in fear and the belief that I was not enough on my own.

The night of the conference, after I introduced her and sat down, I felt both shocked and convicted. Convicted because she preached the *exact* same message God had given me. The same scripture and revelation. When she finished, all I could say was, *"She preached my entire message."* Sitting there, it hit me. I was Moses. I had asked for an Aaron. I had looked for someone else to carry what God had already placed in my hand.

God confirmed the message through her, but the assignment was still mine.

That moment changed me. My lack of confidence did not cancel the call. It only delayed my full obedience. God did not need a substitute for my insecurity. He wanted my trust. God equips those He calls. He does not call those who already feel equipped. Our responsibility is not to prove ourselves worthy. It is to rely on Him fully. If God called you, He will sustain you. If He assigned it, He will supply exactly what you need. And if He trusted you with it, He believes in you more than you believe in yourself.

That experience shifted how I approached my second conference. This time was different. I warred in prayer before it ever began. I refused to walk in unprepared. I refused to shrink back. I did not want to repeat what happened the first time, where I silently wrestled with doubt while someone else voiced what God had spoken to me. So I reached out to the women He placed on my heart to speak. I was intentional. I was prayerful. And when it came time for me to share, I shared the word He gave me without hesitation.

I made a decision. I would not allow doubt to silence what God placed in me to birth. I would not look for another Aaron when He had already called me to stand. That conference was about obedience. And for the first time, I felt the difference between hoping I could do it and knowing God would meet me as I did it.

Let me remind you that God is not questioning His choice. He is not second guessing His decision. He is not waiting on someone else to step in. You are the one He chose and what He plans to use is already in your hand.

Encouragement

Your past does not disqualify you. The doubts that try to rise do not get the final say. The insecurity that whispers lies does not have the authority to stop what God has placed on your life.

God has put His Word inside of you. He has trusted you with His authority, and He has promised His presence every step of the way. You are not moving forward in your own strength. You are equipped because He is with you and when God is with you, lack, fear, and hesitation lose their power.

Affirmations

I am confident in the God who called me.

I trust His choice, even when I question myself.

I am equipped for the assignment before me.

I rely on God, not my own strength.

What God placed in me will be released at the appointed time.

You have what it takes because God is the one who called you. Now trust Him enough to move forward.

Faith in Motion

Before you move forward, take a moment to confront what has been quietly holding you back.

- Name the fear or insecurity that has been holding you back.
- Write down one lie you've believed about yourself and replace it with truth.
- Show up today even if confidence feels shaky.

Prayer

God, I bring my doubts and insecurities to You. I will not hide them. Silence every voice that tells me I am not enough. Quiet comparison, past failures, and fear of being seen. Help me trust that if You chose me, it was intentional. Replace every lie I have believed with Your truth. Teach me to see myself the way You see me.

Strengthen my confidence through obedience. Help me show up even when I feel unsure. Establish my identity in You so deeply that insecurity cannot shake it. I choose to believe what You say about me. I choose to move forward today. In Jesus' name, Amen.

Pause Here

Pause. Breathe. Ask God what He says about you, not what fear says.

It's
Time
TO
SHOW UP

CHAPTER 4

The Cost of Not Showing Up

Sometimes we show up, but not in the fullness of who we are. We present a *representative*. The version that feels more controlled and less exposed. We share what feels manageable, what won't cost us too much, and we keep the rest tucked away. Little by little, we start offering pieces of ourselves instead of our whole selves. And if we're being honest, that isn't really showing up at all.

When we do this, it impacts the people we are called to. They receive fragments instead of fullness. Presenting ourselves means all of us, not just the parts that feel confident or comfortable. Jesus said we are the light of the world, and light is meant to shine, not be hidden (Matthew 5:14–16). When we dim our light, the impact God intended is reduced. You might as well say we are still not showing up.

Then there are times when we do not show up at all. No representative. No presence. Just absence. There is a real cost to hiding, and it is not always immediate. There were seasons when I did not show up fully, not out of rebellion, but hesitation. I knew what God was asking, yet fear and overthinking slowed my obedience. What I did not understand then was how much was attached to my yes.

When I delayed, opportunities expired. Doors that were once open quietly closed because timing matters with obedience. Some things are grace for now, not later. My confidence weakened as well. Confidence is built through obedience, and when movement is avoided, insecurity grows. What God intended to strengthen through action, fear tried to weaken through delay.

Momentum stalled. Vision needs motion to stay alive. When movement slows, clarity fades. The fire that once burned strong began to flicker because it was not being exercised. When purpose is not practiced, it can start to feel distant, even when it is still present.

The most sobering truth was this. People went without what I was called to offer. My hesitation was never just about me. There were answers, encouragement, direction, and provision tied to my willingness to show up. Scripture calls us ambassadors for Christ (2 Corinthians 5:20). When an ambassador does not show up, the message is delayed.

Our absence creates ripple effects. Obedience does not only impact our lives. It affects everyone connected to the assignment God placed in our hands. *"Therefore, to him who knows to do good and does not do it, to him it is sin"* (James 4:17). Once God makes something clear, staying neutral is no longer an option. Choosing not to act is still a choice.

Jonah's story is a prime example. God gave him a direct assignment and Jonah chose not to show up. His delay did not cancel the call, but it created unnecessary consequences. A storm came and others were affected. Not only that, Jonah ended up in the belly of a fish because God was committed to getting him back to the assignment. When Jonah finally obeyed, the impact was immediate. An entire city repented and lives were changed. Delayed obedience does not cancel the assignment, but it often makes the journey harder than it needs to be.

God is faithful and intentional. He knows what is tied to your yes and who is waiting on your obedience. That is why hiding comes at a cost. Fear convinces us that staying back is safer, but obedience is where protection and purpose meet. The enemy does not always have to stop you. Sometimes he just needs to slow you down.

If you feel conviction, receive it as an invitation. God is not angry with you. He is calling you forward. Your yes matters more than you realize.

Encouragement

This is not the season to hide. The grace to move forward is available to you right now. What you thought you missed has not passed you by. Nothing about your life is behind schedule when God is involved.

Momentum is being restored. Confidence is being renewed. Assignments that were delayed were never denied. What felt paused is being reactivated, and clarity is catching up with obedience. Step forward. As you do, you will begin to see God's hand move swiftly and intentionally on your behalf.

Affirmations

I choose obedience over delay.

I show up fully in what God has called me to do.

My obedience releases impact and purpose.

I do not hide from responsibility or calling.

What God entrusted to me will be completed in His timing.

If you have been holding back, let this be your turning point. Showing up is not about perfection. It is about faithfulness. And faithfulness always produces fruit.

Faith in Motion

Before you move any further, take an honest look at what hesitation has been stealing from you.

- Reflect on where delay has cost you momentum.
- Ask God who might be impacted by your obedience.
- Take one action today that interrupts procrastination.

Prayer

God, I choose to stop hiding. I choose to show up fully with what You have placed in my hand. Forgive me for the times I delayed when You were calling me forward. Forgive me for mistaking fear for wisdom and hesitation for preparation. I trust that obedience will produce what confidence alone cannot. Remind me that movement creates clarity. Break the cycle of procrastination and give me discipline to act. Where I have lost momentum, restore it. Where I have felt stuck, shift me. Show me who is connected to my yes. Reveal the lives, opportunities, and impact that are waiting on my obedience. Let that awareness strengthen my resolve.

Help me move forward, even when I feel stretched. Give me courage to take the next step, not the entire staircase. Anchor me in trust and teach me to respond quickly when You speak. I will not hide what You have entrusted to me. I will steward it. I will act on it. I will move. In Jesus' name, Amen.

Pause Here

Pause. Consider what is waiting on the other side of your yes.

It's
Time
TO
SHOW UP

CHAPTER 5

The Decision to Go Forward

You have made it this far, and now it is time to make a decision. A decision is a settled choice. It is not a feeling. It is not an intention. It is a deliberate act of the will. Decisions shape direction, and direction determines movement. At some point, clarity has to turn into choice.

God does not force us to do anything. He never has. He gives instruction, invitation, and direction, but He also gives us something powerful called volition. Volition is the ability to choose. It is the God given capacity to decide. This matters because obedience is only obedience when it is chosen. God desires willing partners, not coerced participants. Your yes carries weight because you are free to say no.

The decision to go forward in obedience takes courage and boldness. That is why Scripture consistently reminds us to be bold and courageous. God does not give that instruction without reassurance. Over and over, He reminds us that He is with us. "Be strong and of good courage. Do not be afraid, nor be dismayed, for the Lord your God is with you wherever you go" (Joshua 1:9). The question becomes simple. Do you believe that? And if you do, what other confirmation are you waiting for?

For a long time, I thought that once God gave me the Word, that was it. I believed hearing Him was the finish line. But hearing God is only the beginning. Obedience is what activates what He has spoken.

If you think back to the previous chapter where I shared about my first conference, I did make the decision to go forward. I gathered everything. I planned. I organized. I moved. But I also made that decision with hesitation. I allowed someone else to speak for me. I was bold enough to execute the assignment, but I was not confident enough to fully trust that God could use my voice. I went forward, but not fully. Looking back, I can see the tension clearly. I moved in obedience, but I held back in belief.

That experience showed me something important. Boldness is not always loud. Sometimes it is quiet movement mixed with insecurity. But God does not just call us to move forward. He calls us to move forward fully.

This is where we need to take on the boldness of David. David did not ignore the giant standing before him. He just refused to be intimidated by it. He did not measure the battle by the size of Goliath. He measured it by the God who was backing him. David remembered who had prepared him for that moment. He remembered the lion. He remembered the bear. He remembered God's faithfulness in private places.

David did not run away from Goliath. He did the opposite. Scripture tells us he ran toward him. That detail matters. He did not slowly walk. He did not hesitate. He moved with decision.

By David standing up, everything shifted. Fear lost its grip on the nation of Israel. A stalemate ended. The people who had been hiding found courage. Victory was released not just for David, but for an entire nation. One person's decision to go forward changed the atmosphere for everyone connected to the battle.

David did not just show up. He was bold enough to slay the giant that so many others were afraid to face. And that victory became evidence. Proof. A reminder that giants fall when God is trusted.

Think about it. There are people facing situations right now that you have already survived. Someone is stuck in fear. Someone is discouraged in their business. Someone is hoping for a way out of a situation that feels impossible. They need evidence that victory exists on the other side. And you might be the David they need. Your obedience could be the confirmation someone else is praying for.

This is why the decision to go forward matters so much. It is never just about you. It is about who is waiting on the other side of your yes.

So let me encourage you. Do not allow the giants before you to keep you from moving forward. Do not let fear convince you to stay still when

God has already gone ahead of you. You have what you need. God is with you. And boldness will meet you when you decide.

Go forward.

Encouragement

Boldness is rising as you move. You are not being overtaken by fear, and the doubts that once tried to hold you back are losing their voice. What used to intimidate you no longer has the same power over you.

As you step forward, clarity will increase and confidence will follow. Your heart is being strengthened and your steps are being steadied. Keep moving. When you do, you will experience God's power meeting you right where obedience takes place.

Affirmations

I walk boldly in what God has spoken.

I do not wait for confidence. I move in obedience.

Fear no longer controls my decisions.

God strengthens me as I step forward.

Boldness rises in me every time I show up.

You do not need to defeat fear before you move. Move, and fear will lose its power.

Faith in Motion

Before you wait another day for the "right" moment, confront the place where hesitation has been disguising itself as preparation.

- Identify one area where you have been waiting to feel ready.
- Take one bold step without waiting for perfect conditions.
- Speak what God has said out loud, even if your voice shakes.

Prayer

God, I choose movement over fear. I refuse to keep postponing what You have already confirmed. Build boldness in me as I step forward. Not artificial confidence, but courage rooted in trust. Strengthen my heart when doubt tries to resurface. Remind me that readiness is often revealed in motion, not in stillness. Help me stop waiting for ideal circumstances and start responding to Your voice.

As I speak what You have said, steady me. Even if my voice trembles, let my faith stand firm. Establish me in truth. Anchor me in obedience. Grow my confidence each time I take a step. I trust You with the outcome. I trust You with the process. I trust You with every step I take. In Jesus' name, Amen.

Pause Here

Pause. Ask yourself, what would boldness look like today?

It's
Time
TO
SHOW UP

CHAPTER 6

Serving as a Member of the Family of Faith

Being part of the body of Christ carries weight. Whether you lead a business, serve in ministry, work a job, raise a family, or support someone else's vision, the standard is the same. What God places in your hands belongs to Him first. I had to shift my mindset. I stopped seeing myself as the owner and started seeing myself as a steward. That one change reshaped everything for me. It changed how I make decisions, how I treat people, and how I approach responsibility. When you realize you are managing what belongs to God, you move differently. You slow down. You pray more. You take things seriously.

1 Corinthians 4:2 says, *"For it is required in stewards that one be found faithful."*

That is not just a word for CEOs. That is a word for believers. Faithfulness is the standard in the Kingdom. One of the hardest lessons I learned was that I could not measure success the way the world does. I tried. I watched what others were doing. I adjusted what God originally showed me because I thought I needed to mirror what looked successful. That decision cost me.

During my first year in business, I did not secure a single client. *Not one.* I questioned everything. I wondered if I heard God correctly. I even thought about walking away. What I eventually realized was I was trying to build a Kingdom assignment using someone else's blueprint. I was applying worldly measurements to something that required spiritual alignment.

When God revealed that to me, I had to repent and realign. I laid everything down and went back to Him. I asked for His blueprint. Once alignment was restored, things shifted. Opportunities opened. Clients came. Most of them came through word of mouth from people I had already served. That was confirmation for me. When you build His way, He sustains it His way. This goes beyond business. If you do not know how to navigate your current season, go back to God. Pray. Seek Him. Ask for His instructions. He is not hiding direction from you. He is waiting for you to seek alignment.

Faithfulness became my anchor. That meant choosing integrity when no one was watching. It meant praying before making decisions. There were times when logic told me to move quickly, but when I prayed, I sensed God telling me to slow down. I learned that hearing Him clearly matters more than moving fast. Speed without Him can create damage that obedience could have prevented.

Stewardship also changed how I treated people. God reminded me that people are not stepping stones. They are souls. Whether authors, clients, church members, partners, or family, how I treated them reflected the One I serve.

It matters how you speak.
It matters how you respond.
It matters how you handle conflict.
It matters how you honor others.

We cannot claim Christ publicly and misrepresent Him privately. Private obedience sustains public influence. What happens behind closed doors shows up in how you lead and serve in front of others. That is why I became intentional about inviting God into every area of my work and life. Prayer stopped being optional. It became necessary. Prayer, integrity, humility, and accountability are not extras in the Kingdom. They are foundational. Without them, influence becomes performance. With them, it becomes fruitful.

Joseph's life speaks to this. Before he stood before Pharaoh, he stewarded Potiphar's house faithfully. When he was placed in prison, he stewarded that space with the same excellence. Long before elevation came, integrity was established.

Daniel is another example. He served in a secular system but refused to compromise his devotion to God. His influence did not come from position alone. It came from consistency. God honored him publicly because he honored God privately.

These stories remind me that Kingdom leadership is not about title. It is about faithfulness wherever God places you. Every decision carries weight. Financial choices matter. Relationships matter. Timing matters. Even knowing when to speak and when to remain silent matters. There were moments when saying no protected me. There were times when slowing down kept me from costly mistakes.

Faithfulness does not always come with applause, but it always has heaven's approval. If you are part of the body of Christ, understand this. God is watching how you steward what He placed in your hands. He cares about how you treat people. He cares about how you respond under pressure. He cares about whether you seek Him before you move. Leadership without stewardship becomes dangerous. Stewardship grounded in faithfulness becomes powerful.

Scriptures to Anchor You

"Trust in the Lord with all your heart, and lean not on your own understanding; in all your ways acknowledge Him, and He shall direct your paths."

Proverbs 3:5–6

"He who is faithful in what is least is faithful also in much."

Luke 16:10

Encouragement for the Family of Faith

You were trusted with this season for a reason. God saw your heart before He entrusted you with responsibility. He is not asking you to impress people. He is asking you to steward well. Serve with integrity. Pray before you decide. Care for the people connected to your assignment. Honor God in private and in public. Faithfulness will carry you farther than talent ever could. You are not defined by a title. You are a steward. You are a representative of Christ. Live like it.

Encouragement

You were entrusted with this assignment because faithfulness was already evident in the hidden places. God saw how you handled pressure, how you treated people, and how you kept seeking Him even when no one was applauding or watching. This is not a random calling, and it is not a mistake. You do not need to question why you were chosen. Grace has been placed on your stewardship, and authority rests on your leadership.

You are learning how to lead without striving and how to make decisions without fear. What you honor in private, God will defend in public. As you steward people with care and integrity, trust will begin to surround you naturally. Your steps are being ordered, your discernment is being sharpened, and what has been placed in your hands is being sustained by God Himself. This is a season of steady growth, divine alignment, and Kingdom influence. Stay faithful. Stay focused. You are not walking alone.

Affirmations

I lead with integrity and humility.

I steward what God has entrusted to me with wisdom and care.

I make decisions prayerfully and confidently.

I honor God publicly and privately.

I am faithful in small things and trusted with more.

God orders my steps and sharpens my discernment.

I am equipped to lead with clarity and courage.

What God placed in my hands will prosper under His guidance.

Faith in Motion

Before you move into your next decision, pause and check your posture.

- Pray before making your next decision.
- Evaluate how you steward people, time, and resources.
- Choose integrity even when no one is watching.

Prayer

God, before I move, I want to hear You clearly. Slow me down where I need to pause and strengthen me where I need to stand firm. Help me lead with integrity and humility in every area of my life. Teach me to steward what You have placed in my hands with wisdom and care. Show me where I have been careless with time, distracted with priorities, or insensitive with people. Refine my heart so that my leadership reflects Your character.

Let my private decisions align with my public declarations. Guard me from pride, impatience, and compromise. When no one is watching, remind me that You are. When shortcuts look appealing, anchor me in truth. May every choice I make honor You. May my life speak louder than my title. May my stewardship bring You glory. In Jesus' name, Amen.

Pause Here

Pause. Reflect on how faithfulness is shaping your leadership.

It's
Time
TO
SHOW UP

CHAPTER 7

When God Calls You For Such a Time as This

There are moments in business and leadership when God accelerates responsibility. Seasons when what once felt optional suddenly becomes urgent. Times when staying quiet is no longer neutral and hiding is no longer an option. You can feel the shift. What you used to postpone starts pressing on your heart. What you once felt comfortable sitting with now demands a response.

Those moments are uncomfortable, but they are intentional. They usually arrive when God is ready to move through you in a bigger way. When He's ready to stretch your obedience, deepen your trust, and expand your impact.

Scripture captures this kind of moment perfectly in the story of Esther:

"Yet who knows whether you have come to the kingdom for such a time as this?"
— Esther 4:14

Esther didn't step into her position by accident. She was chosen, positioned, and prepared, even though she didn't fully understand it at first. Her purpose was connected to timing. The call required courage and her response mattered not just for her own life, but for an entire people.

At first, Esther hesitated. She understood the risk. Speaking up could cost her everything. Remaining silent felt safer. Silence often feels safer when obedience requires visibility. But Mordecai reminded her of a truth we all eventually have to face. If she stayed silent, deliverance would still come, but she would miss her moment to be part of it. That's a sobering thought.

God's plans are bigger than us, but His invitations are personal. He doesn't need us, but He chooses us. And when He does, our response matters. I've learned that visibility isn't about ego. God doesn't elevate us so we can be seen. He positions us so His will can be done. When God places you in rooms, on platforms, or in positions of influence, it's never just for exposure. It's because something needs to be released through you.

Jesus is the ultimate example of this truth. He knew His purpose. He understood the weight of His assignment. He also understood the cost. In the Garden of Gethsemane, Jesus wrestled openly with what obedience would require. He prayed honestly. He asked if there was another way. He didn't pretend the weight wasn't heavy. Yet He surrendered fully to the Father's will.

"Nevertheless not My will, but Yours, be done."
— Luke 22:42

Jesus embraced obedience. His response to the call changed the course of humanity. His willingness to show up, even when it was painful, reminds us that purpose often demands sacrifice. Both Esther and Jesus teach us something powerful. Purpose comes with responsibility and obedience often asks us to step forward when fear would rather keep us quiet. I've experienced moments like this in my own journey. Times when God made it clear that staying silent was no longer an option. Moments when I realized that shrinking back would cost more than stepping forward. When

God calls you for such a time as this, He is inviting your obedience. He's trusting you with influence, timing, and impact.

"For we walk by faith, not by sight."
— 2 Corinthians 5:7

Encouragement

This is your moment. You have been positioned carefully and intentionally, not by accident or delay. Now is not the time to shrink back. What God is asking of you is aligned with His timing, and He does not rush or miss a step.

Your courage is being strengthened, and your heart is being steadied. As you move forward, you are covered. Obedience will open doors, bring freedom, and make room for God's glory to be revealed through your yes.

Affirmations

I am positioned for such a time as this.

I choose obedience over fear.

I show up boldly when God calls me forward.

My visibility serves God's purpose, not my ego.

God strengthens me to respond with faith and courage.

Reflection Questions

- Where has God been nudging me to speak or step forward?
- What fear has been keeping me silent?
- Who might be impacted by my obedience?
- What would change if I trusted God with this moment?

When God calls you for such a time as this, it is not by accident.

Faith in Motion

Before you talk yourself out of it again, pause and recognize that this moment is not random.

- Identify where God is calling you to be visible.
- Speak up in one area where you've been silent.
- Respond to the assignment instead of shrinking back.

Prayer

God, I recognize this moment as intentional. You are not asking me to step forward by accident. You are inviting me into something purposeful. Give me courage to respond with obedience and trust. Where I have hidden out of fear, strengthen me. Where I have stayed silent to stay comfortable, stir boldness in me. Help me stop minimizing what You placed inside of me. Remind me that visibility is not about attention. It is about alignment.

I choose faith over fear. I choose purpose over comfort. I choose obedience over hesitation. Establish my steps as I move forward and give me peace as I respond. In Jesus' name, Amen.

Pause Here

Pause. Ask God if this is your moment to step forward.

It's
Time
TO
SHOW UP

Chapter 8

Faith Requires Action

Remember the Scripture we talked about earlier, the one that says when you know what to do and choose not to do it, it becomes sin (James 4:17). This is where faith has to move beyond agreement and into action. This is where believing turns into obedience. Faith can't stay theoretical. It has to be lived out.

For a long time, I thought faith was mostly about agreement. Agreeing with God. Nodding yes in prayer. Feeling encouraged when a word confirmed what I already hoped was true. But real faith doesn't stop there. Faith moves. Faith responds. Faith shows up.

"Now faith is the substance of things hoped for, the evidence of things not seen."
— Hebrews 11:1

Substance means there's something tangible connected to what you believe. Evidence means there's something visible attached to what you say you trust God for. In other words, faith has a body. It takes shape through action. God honors steps, even imperfect ones. He's not asking for flawless execution. He's asking for obedience. He responds to movement, not perfection.

So many of us believe deeply, pray consistently, and hope sincerely, yet hesitate to move. We want clarity before we act, but God often gives clarity as we act. We want certainty before we step, but God meets us in the stepping.

When I finally took steps, even small ones, momentum followed. Fear started to quiet. Direction became clearer. Faith grew legs. What once felt intimidating became manageable once I moved.

The Bible is full of people who moved before everything made sense. Abraham is one of the clearest examples. God told him to leave his country, his family, and everything familiar without giving him a detailed plan. Abraham obeyed anyway. He moved without knowing where he was going, trusting the One who sent him.

"By faith Abraham obeyed when he was called to go out to the place which he would receive as an inheritance."

— Hebrews 11:8

Abraham's faith showed up through movement. His obedience created space for God to fulfill the promise. Peter's story speaks loudly here too. When Jesus called him to step out of the boat and walk on water, Peter didn't wait for conditions to change. He moved at the word of Jesus. The moment he stepped out, faith became visible.

"So He said, 'Come.' And when Peter had come down out of the boat, he walked on the water to go to Jesus."
— Matthew 14:29

Peter walked because he trusted the voice that called him. Staying in the boat may feel safe, but it limits what you get to experience with God.

The woman with the issue of blood shows us this truth too. She believed Jesus could heal her, but belief alone didn't change her situation. She pressed through the crowd. She reached out. Her faith moved her body.

"If only I may touch His clothes, I shall be made well."
— Mark 5:28

Her action activated her miracle.

These stories remind me that faith isn't passive. Faith partners with God through obedience. Faith says yes and takes a step, even when fear is present. I had to learn that waiting for fear to leave only kept me stuck. Moving despite fear is what allowed my faith to grow. Every time I showed up anyway, faith became more real. Every step made God's presence more tangible.

Encouragement

You are being invited to take a step, even if it feels small. Movement matters, and obedience does not have to be loud to be powerful. As you move, clarity and strength will meet you. Fear will not overtake you, and doubt will not stop you. Your obedience is being honored, and your steps are being established. What you move toward in faith will begin to respond to you.

Affirmations

I walk by faith and not by sight.

My faith moves me to action.

God honors every obedient step I take.

I trust God even when I cannot see the outcome.

As I move, my faith grows stronger.

Faith shows up. And when you show up in faith,
God always meets you there.

Faith in Motion

Before you pray about it again, ask yourself if God is waiting on you to move.

- Write down one step of faith you've been avoiding.
- Move forward even without full clarity.
- Act on what you've been praying about.

Prayer

God, I refuse to let my faith remain stagnant. I do not want to keep circling the same place when You are calling me forward. Give me courage to take the step I have been delaying. Even when the outcome feels unclear, anchor me in what You already said. Teach me to trust Your voice more than my need for details. Break hesitation off my life and strengthen my resolve to act. As I move in faith, meet me with Your direction. Order my steps. Guard my heart. Remind me that You honor obedience. I trust You enough to move. In Jesus' name, Amen.

Pause Here

Pause. What action is faith asking of you right now?

It's
Time
TO
SHOW UP

Chapter 9

Continue to Do the Work

One of the most important lessons I've learned as a CEO is that consistency is essential. Anyone can show up once, have a great idea, a strong launch, or a powerful moment. But leadership is revealed over time. What builds trust isn't a single appearance. It's presence. It's follow through. It's showing up again and again, even when it's inconvenient, uncomfortable, or unseen.

Consistency builds trust with people and with God.

People are watching how we lead. They're paying attention to whether our words line up with our actions. They notice whether we disappear when things get hard or remain steady when pressure shows up. Trust isn't built in big moments alone. It's built in small, repeated acts of faithfulness.

"And let us not grow weary while doing good, for in due season we shall reap if we do not lose heart."

— Galatians 6:9

Don't grow weary. Don't stop showing up. Don't abandon the work just because the results are taking longer than you expected. Due season comes, but it's connected to endurance. Showing up once can inspire people. Showing up continually is what makes you a leader.

As a CEO, consistency matters because vision requires stability. People can't follow leadership that keeps changing direction. They can't trust leadership that only appears during launches, big moments, or breakthroughs. I had to learn that being visible only when things were exciting wasn't enough. Leadership requires presence in the process, not just the highlight reel.

Consistency showed up in my life through prayer, planning, communication, and obedience. There were seasons when I wasn't motivated. Times when I questioned whether my efforts were making any difference at all. But consistency kept the door open for God to work. Even when I couldn't see immediate results, staying steady allowed God to move behind the scenes.

The Bible gives us strong examples of consistent leadership. Noah is one that always stands out to me. God gave him a clear assignment to build the ark. There was no applause. No instant reward.

No visible sign that rain was coming. Yet Noah showed up day after day and built consistently. His obedience over time saved his family and preserved life.

"Thus Noah did; according to all that God commanded him, so he did."
— Genesis 6:22

Daniel is another powerful example. His consistency in prayer never wavered, even when it became dangerous. He prayed three times a day, just as he always had. His commitment to God didn't change when pressure increased. And that consistency honored God and ultimately protected him.

"He knelt down on his knees three times that day, and prayed and gave thanks before his God, as was his custom since early days."
— Daniel 6:10

Jesus Himself modeled consistency. He withdrew to pray regularly. He taught faithfully.

He showed up for people day after day. His consistency in private sustained His power in public. What people saw openly was rooted in what He practiced quietly.

Consistency means commitment. It means deciding ahead of time that you won't quit when progress feels slow or invisible. It's choosing to stay steady even when emotions fluctuate.

As CEOs, we have to understand that consistency protects momentum. It keeps vision alive. It builds confidence in the people we lead. It also deepens our trust in God, because we learn to rely on Him daily, not just in moments of crisis.

There were times when I wanted to pause or pull back simply because I was tired. But every time I stayed consistent, I watched God move in ways I couldn't have planned. Consistency kept me aligned when my emotions tried to pull me off course.

"He who is faithful in what is least is faithful also in much."

— Luke 16:10

Encouragement

If you're weary, don't stop. If you're discouraged, stay the course. God sees your faithfulness, even when it feels unseen by others. The harvest you're praying for is tied to your endurance. Consistency may not be glamorous, but it is powerful. It's doing more than you realize. Show up again. Show up steady. Show up trusting God. What you are faithful with today is quietly building the future you will walk into tomorrow.

Affirmations

I show up consistently, not occasionally.

I lead with faithfulness, not feelings.

My consistency builds trust and credibility.

I remain steady even when results feel delayed.

God honors my endurance and obedience.

I do not grow weary in doing good.

My faithfulness positions me for harvest.

I am committed to the work God entrusted to me.

I lead with clarity, courage, and consistency.

What God started through me will be completed.

Faith in Motion

Before you wait for motivation to return, make a decision that does not depend on how you feel.

- Commit to one habit that supports consistency.
- Show up this week even if motivation is low.
- Remind yourself why consistency matters.

Prayer

God, help me remain steady and faithful. Teach me not to be led by emotion but anchored in discipline. When I feel weary, renew my strength. When I feel distracted, refocus my heart. Remind me that small, consistent steps produce lasting fruit. Guard me from starting strong and fading quickly. Build endurance in me so I can keep showing up even when no one applauds. Help me trust You for the harvest while I commit to the process. Let my faithfulness reflect my trust in You. In Jesus' name, Amen.

Pause Here

Pause. Ask yourself where God is calling you to remain consistent.

It's
Time
TO
SHOW UP

Chapter 10

Already Started But Stalled

You showed up. I need you to sit with that for a second before we go any further. You heard God, you pulled together your courage, and you moved. You launched the business, stepped into the ministry, said yes to the assignment, or took that first real step toward the vision He put in your heart. That was not a small thing. Obedience always costs something, and you paid it, but somewhere between that beginning and where you thought you would be by now, something changed. The momentum got quiet. The clarity that used to feel sharp started getting fuzzy. Life came at you. Disappointment moved in and got comfortable. You kept showing up for a while, going through the motions, but if you are being real with yourself right now, the fire is not burning the way it was. You stalled and if that is where you are, I need you to hear me on this. Stalling is not the same as failing. It is not the same as being done.

There is a real difference between someone who quit and someone who paused. Quitting is a decision that happens in the heart. Stalling is usually a signal. It is God getting your attention, slowing things down long enough for you to catch your breath and recalibrate. So the question is not whether you stalled. Most people reading this have. The real question is what you are going to do now that you can see it.

You Are Not the First

Scripture is full of people who started strong and then went quiet. Elijah called down fire from heaven, and then turned around and sat under a tree asking God to take his life. He was worn out, overwhelmed, and fully convinced the assignment was finished. But God did not pull the calling off of him. He sent an angel with food and told him to rest. Then He spoke to Elijah again. Not in the fire, not in the earthquake, but in a still small voice. And He sent him right back to the work.

What I find powerful about that story is that God did not rebuke Elijah for stopping. He took care of him first. He tended to the physical exhaustion before He addressed the spiritual direction. So sometimes when you stall, God is not standing over you frustrated. He is right there tending to you. He is replenishing what the journey took out of you. The pause was not punishment. It was preparation for what is still ahead.

Then there is Nehemiah. He was rebuilding the wall and people were coming against him from every direction. The workers got tired. The threats kept coming. Morale started dropping. But Nehemiah did not pretend none of that was happening. He dealt with it. He reorganized. He put people where they were strongest and reminded them of what they were actually fighting for. He did not make the people feel bad for being tired. He gave them a reason to pick their tools back up.

"Do not be afraid of them. Remember the Lord, great and awesome, and fight for your brethren, your sons, your daughters, your wives, and your houses." —*Nehemiah 4:14*

That one reminder changed everything. They got back to work. Sometimes that is honestly all it takes to restart. You just need to be reminded of why you started in the first place.

Why We Stall

Stalling does not usually happen all at once. It creeps in slowly, and by the time you notice it, it has already been going on for a while. From what I have seen in my own life and in the lives of people I have walked alongside, it tends to come from a few common places. Sometimes it is burnout from carrying the vision alone. You were never supposed to do this without God's daily involvement and the right people around you. When you try to hold everything yourself, exhaustion is going to show up eventually. It is not a character flaw. It is just what happens when you carry more than you were designed to carry alone. Sometimes it is disappointment with how long things are taking. You expected movement by now. When the results did not show up on the timeline you had in your head, discouragement got in quietly and started slowing your steps before you even realized it. Sometimes it is actually fear of the next level. This one surprises people. You can stall not because you are losing momentum, but because you are getting closer to something bigger and fear shows up before obedience can. The closer you get to the breakthrough, the louder the resistance tends to get.

Sometimes it is comparison and confusion. You looked at what someone else was doing and started second-guessing your own lane. What God designed specifically for you started feeling like it was not enough, and somewhere in there you lost your footing trying to walk a path that was never yours to walk, and sometimes it is unprocessed failure or hurt. Something did not go the way you planned, and instead of grieving it and moving through it, you quietly absorbed it as proof that you were not the right person for the assignment.

I know all of these personally. There was a season where I had the vision, I had started the work, and I had seen early signs that God was moving. But I hit a wall. I started questioning whether I was really the right person for what

God was asking me to do. I compared where I was to where others seemed to be. I let a handful of disappointments slowly chip away at my confidence. And before I even realized what had happened, I was showing up in my body but I was not really there. I was going through the motions. That is what stalling from the inside looks like, and it is harder to spot than the kind where you just stop entirely.

God had to take me back to the original word He gave me. He had to remind me that the assignment had not changed just because my circumstances did. The call was still on my life. The only real question was whether I was going to return to it fully.

The Restart Is an Act of Obedience

Getting back up after a stall is not admitting that you failed. It is choosing obedience one more time and God honors that. Think about Jonah. He ran from the assignment completely.

He went in the opposite direction on purpose. He ended up in the belly of a fish. But when he prayed, God heard him. When he turned back toward the assignment, God gave it right back to him. The city still needed what God had put in Jonah. Running from obedience and returning to it are not the same as being disqualified from it.

Think about Peter. He denied Jesus three times, and shame could have had him convinced that he was done. But Jesus went looking for him personally. He did not just offer Peter a general pardon and move on. He restored him in a very specific way. Three times He asked, do you love Me? Three times Peter said yes. And three times Jesus handed the assignment back. Feed My lambs. Tend My sheep. The calling came back with the restoration.

"So when they had eaten breakfast, Jesus said to Simon Peter, 'Simon, son of Jonah, do you love Me more than these?' He said to Him, 'Yes,

Lord; You know that I love You.' He said to him, 'Feed My lambs.'" —*John 21:15*

God is not finished with you because you stalled. He is inviting you back to the assignment the same way He invited Peter back. With grace, with purpose, and with a very clear next step.

How to Restart

Restarting is not about coming up with a whole new plan. It is about returning to the original one with a fresh surrender. Here is what that actually looks like: *Go back to the word God gave you. Pull out the journal entry, find the note in your phone, go back to the prayer you prayed when it all first became clear. Read it again. Let it remind you that this vision was His before it was ever yours, and He has not taken it back.*

Be honest with God about where you have been. Not with shame, just with honesty. Tell Him what happened. He already knows, but there is something powerful about naming it out loud to Him. Repentance is not about beating yourself up. It is about realignment. It is turning back toward the direction He pointed and saying out loud that you are ready to move again.

Name what caused the stall. Was it burnout? Disappointment? Fear of what the next level requires? You cannot deal with what you have not named. Sit with it long enough to understand it, then bring it to God specifically rather than in general terms.

Take one step. Not ten steps. Not a full relaunch. Just one faithful step in the direction God originally called you. Momentum gets rebuilt the same way it got built the first time, one act of obedience followed by another, day after day.

Get someone around you. You may have stalled partly because you were doing this alone. Find someone who will ask you the hard questions, pray with you, and hold you to what God said. Isolation and momentum do not coexist for long.

Your Stall Did Not Disqualify You

I want to say this one more time because I know someone reading this really needs to let it settle in. The fact that you stalled does not mean you missed God. It does not mean the assignment has moved to someone else. It does not mean the window closed while you were not looking.

What God spoke over your life before you ever took that first step is still true. The people who are connected to your obedience are still out there waiting. The impact that was tied to your yes has not expired. God does not operate on your timeline, and His patience with you is not the same thing as Him withdrawing from you. He is not somewhere in the distance watching to see if you can pull yourself together. He is close. He is still speaking. He is ready to walk back into the assignment with you the moment you turn toward it.

The stall was a chapter in the story, not the ending of it. What God started in you is still alive and it is waiting on your return. So get back up. Pick up what you set down. The work is still yours.

Encouragement

The fact that you stalled does not erase what God said. His word over your life did not expire while you were catching your breath. The vision He placed in you is still valid. The people connected to your assignment are still waiting. The grace to finish what He started in you is still available right now. You have not missed your moment. You are standing in it. This is the moment of return, and God is meeting you here with the same patience, the same purpose, and the same call He placed on your life from the beginning. Get back up. The assignment is still yours.

Affirmations

I am not disqualified by the pause.

I return to the assignment with a fresh surrender.

God's word over my life has not expired.

I take one faithful step today.

What God started in me will be completed.

I choose obedience over shame.

My restart is an act of faith, not an admission of defeat.

God is with me as I return to the work.

Faith in Motion

Before you wait until you feel completely ready, make one move today that shows God you are turning back toward the assignment.

- Go back to the original word or vision God gave you and read it again this week.
- Name the one thing that caused the stall and bring it to God honestly in prayer, by name, not in general.
- Identify one concrete step you can take this week to re-engage the assignment,

even if it feels small.

Prayer

God, I am coming back to You. Not with a perfect record, but with a willing heart. I want to be honest with You about where I have been. I let things slow me down. I let disappointment take root. I let fear and weariness pull me off course. I am not making excuses for any of it. I am just returning. Forgive me for the times I let the weight of the journey convince me that the assignment was over. Forgive me for comparing my progress to other people and losing sight of the lane You designed specifically for me. Forgive me for letting silence become comfortable when You were calling me forward the whole time.

I am picking back up what I put down. I am returning to the vision You gave me. I trust that Your word has not expired and that the impact tied to my obedience is still very much alive. Restore my momentum. Renew my faith. Remind me every day of the why behind the work. Bring the right people around me who will speak truth and hold me accountable. As I take the next step, meet me there. Order my steps. Guard my heart from every voice that told me to stay down. I am choosing to get back up today. In Jesus' name, Amen.

Pause Here

Pause. Ask God what returning fully to the assignment looks like for you today.

It's
Time
TO
SHOW UP

CHAPTER 11

It's Time to Show Up, Now Walk it Out

Everything you've read up to this point has been preparing you for right now. Not to hype you up for a moment, but to move you into action. Not just to stir your emotions, but to shape your obedience. This is where it stops being information and becomes personal. You don't need another confirmation. You don't need permission from anyone. You don't need to feel ready. God already spoke.

Here's a Scripture I rely on mostly as a CEO:

"Have I not commanded you? Be strong and of good courage; do not be afraid, nor be dismayed, for the Lord your God is with you wherever you go." — Joshua 1:9

God didn't say wait until you feel strong. He said be strong. Courage isn't a feeling you chase. It's a decision you make when you trust the One who sent you. From the very beginning, God made it clear that you weren't just called to believe Him. You were called to build with Him. That meant your yes came with responsibility, participation, and follow through. Belief was never meant to stop at agreement. It was always meant to move you into action.

Along the way, you had to confront the confidence struggle most people never talk about. The enemy tried to use your past, your doubts, and your questions to make you wonder if God chose the right person. But what you learned is this. God doesn't make accidental selections. He knew your weaknesses when He called you. He wasn't surprised by your history. Your assignment was never to prove yourself worthy. It was to trust His choice.

You also had to face the cost of not showing up. You saw that hesitation doesn't just affect you. It slows momentum. It delays impact. It leaves people waiting on what you were called to release. God wasn't condemning you. He was inviting you forward. Then came the lesson on boldness. You learned that confidence doesn't come before obedience. It comes through it. Every step strengthened your voice. Every decision sharpened your authority. Boldness wasn't something you waited to feel. It was something you built as you moved. You stepped into leadership with a new understanding. Being a CEO in the Kingdom meant more than titles or results. It meant stewardship. It meant praying before deciding, leading with integrity, and honoring God both publicly and privately. Faithfulness became the standard, even when it wasn't flashy or celebrated.

There were moments when God made it clear that silence was no longer an option. Those "such a time as this" moments showed up, and you realized visibility wasn't about ego. It was about obedience. Like Esther, you understood that staying quiet would cost more than stepping forward. Like Jesus, you learned that surrender can feel heavy, but obedience always carries purpose.

Your faith had to move. Agreement wasn't enough anymore. Faith required action. Just like Abraham had to leave, Peter had to step out, and the woman with the issue of blood had to press through, you had to move even when the outcome wasn't fully clear. Faith became visible through your steps. And then there was consistency. You learned that leadership isn't about showing up once. It's about showing up again and again. Consistency built trust. It protected momentum. It positioned you for harvest, even when results took time to appear. All of it points here.

Walking it out means choosing obedience daily. It means no longer negotiating with fear or waiting for perfect conditions. It means trusting that God already factored in every limitation when He entrusted you with the vision.

Let this Scripture encourage you:

"Being confident of this very thing, that He who has begun a good work in you will complete it until the day of Jesus Christ."
— Philippians 1:6

God finishes what He starts. Your role is to stay present while He does the completing.

If you've been questioning yourself, hear this. Moses questioned his ability. Gideon questioned his strength. Jeremiah questioned his age. And God answered all of them the same way. I am with you.

"For it is God who works in you both to will and to do for His good pleasure."
— Philippians 2:13

So take the next step. Not ten steps ahead. Just the next one. God gives light as you move, not before. God trusted you with the vision. Now trust Him enough to show up and walk it out. You're not late. You're not under qualified. You're not forgotten.

It's time to show up.

Encouragement

You were trusted with this vision because God knew you could carry it. There was no confusion when He chose you and no mistake when He placed this assignment in your hands. He accounted for the fears, the questions, and the growth process and still said yes to you.

This is not a season to hesitate or shrink back. This is a season to stand, to move, and to walk it out. God is with you in every step, strengthening your resolve and steadying your heart. What was placed inside of you will not die in delay. It will live through your obedience.

As you show up, doors will open that you could not open on your own. As you remain faithful, your work will be established. As you move forward, God will confirm His word through fruit, clarity, and impact.

Do not look back. Do not second guess. Do not wait for another sign.

This is your moment. Walk in it.

Affirmations

I am chosen and trusted by God.

I show up fully for the assignment He gave me.

I walk in obedience, not fear.

God is with me wherever I go.

I am equipped for what I am called to do.

My steps are ordered and established by the Lord.

I move forward with confidence and faith.

What God started through me will be completed.

Faith in Motion

Before you ask for more confirmation, pause and respond to what He has already made clear.

- Identify your next clear step and commit to it.
- Stop waiting for another sign.
- Choose obedience today.

Prayer

God, I trust You with this next step. You have already spoken, and I do not need another sign to move. Quiet every excuse that tries to delay what You have confirmed. I choose obedience over hesitation and faith over fear. Strengthen me where I feel uncertain. Steady me where I feel stretched. Help me act on what I know instead of stalling for what I do not. As I walk this out, lead me. Establish my steps. Guard my heart from doubt and keep me aligned with Your will. I trust that You go before me and walk with me. In Jesus' name, Amen.

Pause Here

Pause. This is your moment. Let God seal this decision in your heart.

Epilogue

Dear Reader,

I want you to know something before you close this book. Writing it was an act of obedience for me. Every chapter came from a real place, from real moments of fear, hesitation, delay, and eventually surrender. I did not write from a position of having it all figured out. I wrote from the other side of deciding to show up anyway, and I am still learning what that means every single day.

So if you made it to this page, I am proud of you. Not because reading a book is a major accomplishment, but because something in you kept turning the pages even when a chapter hit too close. Even when a question made you uncomfortable. Even when part of you wanted to put it down and come back to it later, which really means never. You stayed. That matters.

I want to speak something over you before you go. You are not behind. I know it can feel that way when you look at how long you have been sitting on the vision God gave you, or when you think about how much time passed while you were working up the courage to move. But God does not measure time the way we do, and He has never once looked at your life and thought you were too late. You are exactly where you need to be to take the next step.

You are not disqualified. Not by your past, not by the season where you stalled, not by the confidence you do not yet feel. God knew every single thing about you before He placed this assignment on your life, and He chose you anyway. That was not a mistake. That was intentional.

You are not alone in this. I know it can feel isolated when you are carrying a vision that not everyone around you understands. I know what it is like to have something burning on the inside that you cannot fully explain to the people closest to you. But God is with you in it. He was there when He gave it to you, and He is here right now as you decide what to do with it.

And the people connected to your yes are still waiting. That is the part I hope stays with you long after you set this book down. Your obedience was never just about you. There are lives, conversations, businesses, ministries, and moments that are tied to your willingness to show up. Every day you delay, someone goes without what you were meant to carry to them. Every day you step forward, something gets released that only you could release in the way God designed.

So here is what I am asking you to do. Do not let this book become something you finished. Let it become something that finished something in you. The hesitation. The excuse. The waiting for the right moment that never feels like it arrives. Let this be the page where that ends.

You already know what God told you to do. You have known for a while. And I believe that is exactly why this book found its way into your hands. Not by accident. Not by coincidence. But because the God who entrusted you with a vision is still calling you forward, and He will use whatever it takes to get your attention. Consider this your reminder. Consider this your push. Consider this your permission, if that is what you needed, to stop waiting and start walking.

It is time to show up. For real this time. With your whole heart, with your full obedience, and with the trust that God will meet you in every step you take. I am cheering for you. I am praying for you. And I cannot wait to hear what God does through your yes.

With love and faith,

Shameka Nicole

Now It's Your Turn

If you've made it to this point, it's because something in you knows it's time. Not time to read another book. Not time to wait for another confirmation. Time to move. This book was meant to lead you into action. And while your next step is ultimately between you and God, you don't have to figure it out alone.

But let's be honest about where you are right now. Something shifted as you read these pages. Maybe it was quiet and gradual, building chapter by chapter until the weight of it finally settled. Maybe it hit all at once and you had to put the book down for a minute just to breathe. Either way, something in you is different than it was when you first opened to page one. You feel it. The stirring is louder. The excuses feel thinner. And the thing God has been asking you to do feels less like a possibility and more like a responsibility.

At the same time, you may still be sitting with some things. Maybe there is a fear you named in one of those chapters that you haven't fully handed over yet. Maybe the clarity came but the confidence is still catching up. Maybe you know the next step but the thought of actually taking it still makes your stomach tight. That is okay. That is normal. The gap between knowing and doing is real, and most people try to cross it by themselves in silence, which is exactly how so many assignments stay unfinished.

You don't have to do it that way. Some of you need someone to walk alongside you for this next part. Not to tell you what God already told you, but to help you stop talking yourself out of it. That's what the next two options are for.

For some of you, what you need right now is clarity. You know God has been calling you forward, but you're standing at a decision point and don't want to move blindly. That's where the *Push Forward Activation Call* comes in.

This is a focused, faith-centered conversation designed to help you identify what's been holding you back and clarify your next step. We pray, we listen, and we move forward with intention. This call is for those who are ready to stop circling and start walking.

If you're ready for clarity, confirmation, and movement, scan the QR code to book your session. Don't wait for perfect conditions. Take the next obedient step and move forward.

For others, you know one conversation is not going to be enough. You need accountability. You need structure. You need a space where obedience is supported and consistency is built over time. That's why I created the It's Time to Show Up Mentorship Experience.

This is a small, intimate coaching space for leaders and visionaries who are ready to walk this season out with guidance, prayer, and accountability. This is where showing up becomes a lifestyle, not just a moment.

No matter which path fits you right now, the invitation is the same. Don't ignore the nudge. Don't dismiss the stirring.

If you have questions, need clarity, or want to explore next steps, I'd love to hear from you.

Contact Information

Website:

www.visionairepc.com

Email:

info@visionairepc.com

You can reach out with questions, to inquire about coaching or mentorship, or to learn more about upcoming opportunities.

Thank you for taking this journey with me. My prayer is that these pages didn't just encourage you but positioned you to move.

What happens next is up to you. *But now you know it's time to show up.*

About the Author

Shameka is a faith driven entrepreneur, author, publisher, and visionary leader who is passionate about helping others walk boldly in the assignments God has placed on their lives. She is the founder of Visionaire Publishing & Consulting, a faith centered publishing and consulting company created to help writers, leaders, and visionaries move from calling to completion.

Shameka's journey has been shaped by obedience, resilience, and a deep trust in God. Through years of building businesses, launching initiatives, hosting conferences, and walking out her own faith journey, she has learned firsthand that showing up requires courage, consistency, and dependence on God. Her work is rooted in lived experience, biblical truth, and a heart for stewardship.

As an author and mentor, Shameka equips others to overcome fear, silence doubt, and lead with integrity. She believes that God does not call the equipped, but equips those He calls, and that confidence is built through obedience. Her mission is to help others recognize the value of their yes and step fully into what God has entrusted to them.

Through her books, mentorship programs, and conferences, Shameka continues to encourage others to lead with faith, steward their assignments well, and finish the work God has called them to do.

Connect With Me

Website: www.visionairepc.com

Email: info@visionairepc.com

Facebook: Shameka Raybon + Visionaire Publishing & Consulting

Also by Shameka

Precious Life

Dear Young Woman: There's Triumph After the Trial

Heal HER: A 15 Day Journey from Pain to Promise

Shattered Hearts & Wounded Souls: Our Stories of Survival & Triumph

Woman Arise: Now Is Your Time

It Didn't Break Me, It Built Me: I'm Still Standing

Voices Crying Out

Empower Her: Elevate & Alleviate

I Vow to Pray for My Husband Devotional Prayer Journal

My Salvation Story: His Death = My Freedom Vol. 1 & 2

She Who Hungers... Longing for More of God

Letters to My Sisters: I Lived Through It So You Won't Have To

It's
Time
TO
SHOW UP

www.ingramcontent.com/pod-product-compliance
Lightning Source LLC
LaVergne TN
LVHW020712110826
845149LV00012B/2234

* 9 7 9 8 9 9 4 4 3 1 8 4 9 *